WINNING
COMPETITION AND FAITH

FAST LANE BIBLE STUDIES

by Terry Goertzen

F&L
FAITH&LIFE
P R E S S

Herald
Press

Newton, Kansas
Winnipeg, Manitoba

Scottdale, Pennsylvania
Waterloo, Ontario

Winning: Competition and Faith is a five-session Bible study curriculum that challenges youth and teachers to lessen the negative aspects of competition in their lives, and to emphasize excellence and building up others.

Copyright © 1999 by Faith & Life Press. This publication may not be reproduced, stored in a retrieval system, or transmitted in whole or in part, in any form by any means—electronic, mechanical, photocopying, recording, or otherwise—without prior permission of Faith & Life Press.

Printed in the United States of America
00 99 98 97 4 3 2 1
International Standard Book Number 87303-336-1

Editorial direction for Faith & Life Press by Byron Rempel-Burkholder; editorial consultant, Abe Bergen; editor, Helen H. Johns; copyeditor, Kim Benson; design, Jim L. Friesen; printing by Mennonite Press.

Unless otherwise noted, Scripture text is from the New Revised Standard Version, copyright © 1990, Division of Christian Education of the National Council of Churches in Christ in the United States of America.

TABLE OF CONTENTS

INTRODUCTION

Junior-high youth, like the rest of us, live in a competition-filled world. We see competition in sports, in academics, in families, in friendships, at church, and at work. Everywhere we turn, there is some form of competition, whether acknowledged and accepted, or silently tolerated.

Opinions differ on whether competition is good or bad, helpful or harmful. As Christians who desire to please God in daily life, we will gain insight in this unit about how competition affects us, how we respond to it. Young and old alike, as growing and maturing individuals, can learn to deal with competition in ways that are thoughtful, helpful, and God-honoring.

The stories and writings of Scripture guide us as we examine our attitudes and behaviours. Over the next five sessions your youth will engage in playful competitions that expose attitudes and feelings about the competition they face in real life. You will encourage your youth to learn new ways of treating others. Challenge them to pursue excellence, helpful speech, nonretaliation, service, and Christian community as alternatives to harmful competition.

We hope you enjoy teaching this unit on competition.

"When Competition Kills," based on the story of Cain and Abel (Genesis 4:1-9), will lead youth to the idea that striving for excellence, not beating others, is what pleases God.	**SESSION 1**
The words of the women in 1 Samuel 18:6-16 added to the jealousy and anger Saul felt for David. "Puzzling Popularity" will help youth discover the power their words hold in potentially damaging competitive situations.	**SESSION 2**
Competition at home can cause deep and long-lasting damage to relationships that should be safe and loving. "When Home is Hard" shows that even when competition tears a family apart, reconciliation and wholeness are possible (Genesis 27, 32–33).	**SESSION 3**
"Winning in the Eyes of Jesus" (Luke 22:24-30) will help youth discover that competing for the admiration of others is not the Jesus way. Jesus calls each of us to choose serving others as the path to real joy.	**SESSION 4**
"Adventure Together" will help your youth discover that striving together as teammates will help them succeed as followers of Jesus (Ecclesiastes 4:19-12; Ephesians 3:16-21).	**SESSION 5**

HOW TO | TEACH THIS COURSE

From Life to Bible to Life

The teaching plan used in this study is called life-centered because our teaching begins with a life situation. After discussing a common situation young teens may experience, we search the Scriptures to see what God has to say about the issue. Then we return to the life situation and consider practical applications and age-appropriate responses to the situation.

The Bible is at the center of this study both literally and methodologically. Since we feel the Bible ought to speak to every life issue, it is central to the studies that follow.

USING THE | TEACHER'S GUIDE

PREPARATION

Orient yourself to the lesson by reading through the Preparation section. Here you will find the central focus of the lesson as well as the teaching objective.

Scripture text

The session is rooted in this Bible passage. Read through it to gain a sense of what the text is saying. What strikes you as you read it?

Faith focus

This is the story of the Scripture passage in a nutshell. Here is the nugget of truth on which we will focus this lesson.

Session goal

As you teach, be aware of your goal. What outcomes of this lesson—changes in knowledge, attitude, or action—do you desire in your students?

Materials and advance preparation needed

You will find a list of what you will need to carry through the suggested lesson plan. Glance over this part a week before you teach this lesson.

EXPLORATION

Carefully follow the five step-by-step movements through the lesson. They will carry you from life to the Bible and back to life. The variety of activities should appeal to different kinds of learners and keep your students from getting bored.

1. **Focus.** This movement serves two purposes: to create a friendly climate in the classroom and to focus attention on the session's topic. Usually this beginning step will be interactive and fun.

2. **Connect.** Here the student's experience is connected to the issue. In a variety of ways, students are drawn in to share their experiences as they relate to this topic.

3. **Hear and Enter.** Attention turns to the Bible passage. Students are invited to enter into dialogue with the faith story and explore what it has to say to the questions raised by the issue in the earlier steps. The emphasis is to help students discover new insights about the Scriptures.

4. **Apply.** "So what?" is the question discussed here. How does the Scripture relate to and apply to the issue under consideration?

5. **Respond.** What are the students willing to do as a result of their study? How will their attitudes and actions be different as a result of this study?

REFLECT AND LOOK AHEAD

Evaluative questions help you reflect on the experience of this session. Here are also reminders of what you need to do for the next session.

DIGGING DEEPER

This section provides background and insights for step 3 through additional comments and interpretations of the Scripture text. Read it and let it inspire your teaching.

HANDOUTS

Each session includes activity handouts that may be photocopied and distributed to the students.

JUNIOR HIGH IS NOT A DISEASE!

Just like adults, junior-high youth have their good days and bad days, their ups and downs, and experience a range of feelings and emotions.

Sometimes they feel lonely, frustrated, insecure, moody, happy, anxious, relaxed, confused, determined, and driven.

Sometimes they are bored, competent, capable, delighted, quarrelsome, caring, helpful, indifferent, cautious, optimistic, discouraged, proud, and remorseful. Adults are all those things too.

WHO ARE JUNIOR HIGHS?

Developmentally there are some significant differences between young teens and adults:
•Young teens are just beginning to learn to think and reason abstractly.
•Their attention spans range from four to seven minutes.
•If it takes you more than 1.2 seconds to change activities, you will lose them.
•They are a visual generation. Pictures have replaced words.
•They are active and energetic. Learning must be activity-oriented.
•They are an image generation. They hate to be singled out, made to look stupid, or appear "uncool." They respond well to positive reinforcement.
•They respond in half the time that it takes adults to respond.

Other tips junior high leaders might find helpful:
•Overplan so you do not run out of ideas.
•Develop a "quiet box" with various noisemakers you might use to get their attention.
•Do activities that build up kids' self-esteem rather than forcing them to compete or stand alone.

LEARNING STYLES[1]

Each of us has a special way in which we process or use what we see. This is called our learning style. We learn best when we are taught in ways that complement our learning style.

Where do learning styles come from? Our heredity, past life experiences, the style of a favorite teacher, and the demands of our environment all help create our learning style.

Recent research has shown that there are four main learning styles among North Americans:
•Innovative learners—people who learn by small group interaction and role playing.
•Analytic learners—people who learn through stories and demonstrations.
•Commonsense learners—people who learn by doing.
•Dynamic learners—people who learn by creating.

Effective leaders keep in mind that what is comfortable for them as teachers might not be best for those whose learning styles differ from theirs. No style is right or wrong. We simply learn in different ways. Try to plan at least one activity per session for learners in each of these styles.

[1]The section on learning styles draws from the work of Marlene LeFever in *Creative Teaching Methods* (D.C. Cook, 1985).

SESSION 1

PREPARATION

Scripture texts: Genesis 4:1-9 and Colossians 3:23

Key verse: Whatever your task, put yourselves into it, as done for the Lord. (Colossians 3:23)

Faith focus: God rejected Cain's sacrifice and accepted Abel's. Cain gave in to sin, hating his brother for shedding light on his sacrifice. Cain killed his brother, thus demonstrating the extreme sinfulness humankind is capable of in the face of jealousy born out of competition.

Session goal: Help youth discover their own attitudes about losing and winning, and their possible desire to retaliate when the outcome doesn't go their way. In this discovery, they will realise that doing their best, with the intention of pleasing God, is what God wants.

WHEN COMPETITION KILLS

Materials and advance preparation needed:
- Newspapers and three large boxes, pails, or trashcans (Focus, Option 1)
- Scrap paper and pencils (Focus, Option 2)
- Balloons of two colors, two thumbtacks or stick pins (Focus, Option 3)
- Signs posted around the room, each with one of the following words on it: angry, proud, humble, indifferent, obliged, disappointed, jealous, confused, afraid, winner, loser.
- Handout: "Pleasing God or Spilling Blood" (Hear and Enter)
- Handout: "Charting My Attitudes" (Apply, Option 2)

EXPLORATION

Option 1: If you have a large space, play **Paper Wad Soccer**. Divide into three teams. Don't worry if the teams are unequal in size. Give each team a five-gallon pail, large garbage can, or cardboard box to use as a goal. Again, don't worry if the goals aren't all the same size; this just adds to the tension. Give each team a large section of newspaper and have them create lots of soccer balls out of the paper. Once made, collect the balls, have teams stand behind their goals, and explain the rules for Paper Wad Soccer. **The**

FOCUS
(5 minutes)

object: Have few or no paper wads in your own goal.
The rules: No hands may be used for scoring. Once a paper wad is in a goal, it may not be removed.
Playing the game: Time limit, three minutes; play begins when all the balls are dropped in the center of the playing field.

Option for a smaller space: Play a similar game around a table with players flicking small paper wads or coins with their fingers into goals around the table.

Option 2: Divide into twos or threes. Have each group list on scrap paper times and places in life where competition occurs. Tell youth to be creative. After four minutes have groups share with the larger group their three best ideas.

Option 3: Play **Human Foosball** using balloons as balls and youth as players. Give half the participants several balloons of one color and the other half an equal number of balloons of another color. Each team chooses a goalie. Give goalies a thumbtack or stick pin. Once all the balloons are blown up, have teams sit in rows facing the goal they want to score on. A goal is scored when a balloon hits the wall behind the goalie. Goalies should pop the opposing team's balloons whenever they can. Players must stay seated and goalies may not get off of their knees. If the teaching space is very small, place a height restriction on each goal: Balloons more than five feet up on the wall do not count.

CONNECT
(5 minutes)

Option 1: After a few minutes of Paper Wad Soccer, talk with the group about how they reacted when their goal was scored upon. Ask the group what they saw people say or do when a goal was scored against them. *Did anyone want to retaliate by removing paper wads from the goals even though it was against the rules? Did anyone want to retaliate by trying harder to score on one of the other teams?* Ask: *If I had given the winning team a good prize, how many of you would have been fighting feelings of jealousy?*

Option 2: Tell the group about a time you felt like a loser. Explain briefly how you felt and how you responded. The story can illustrate either a positive response on your part, or one that you know was not right. Ask if there is someone in the group today who would tell about a time they felt like a loser.

Option 3: Say: *A game like Human Foosball is meant to be fun and exciting, regardless of who wins or loses, but sometimes we get caught up in the competition and feel frustrated when things don't turn out the way we want. Can you think of a time you felt frustrated when things didn't go as you had hoped in a competitive situation?* Draw out discussion.

Transition comment: *Competition is a regular part of life for all of us. Sometimes competition can be a good thing, but often we allow winning and losing to become our focus, instead of striving for personal excellence. The first family on earth discovered that competition can create feelings of jealousy and even hatred.*

HEAR AND ENTER
(15 minutes)

Post several signs around the room, each with a different emotion or feeling listed (angry, proud, humble, indifferent, obliged, disappointed, jealous, confused, afraid, winner, loser). Ask four volunteers to read Genesis 4:1-9 (see handout: "Pleasing God or Spilling Blood"). After the reading, have participants stand by one of the signs posted around the room, describing how they might have felt if they were:

- Adam and Eve watching Abel make a good offering,
- Cain watching Abel make a good offering,
- Adam and Eve watching Cain making a not-so-good offering,
- God receiving Cain's not-so-good offering, and
- Cain after being rebuked by God and told to make a choice.

After each scenario, briefly discuss with youth why they chose the feelings they did.

Have a volunteer read Colossians 3:23. Divide into groups of three to five. Have groups act out how Genesis 4:1-9 might have turned out differently if both brothers had striven for excellence in order to make God happy. (Point out that God rebukes Cain mainly for the angry attitude he has allowed to fester after the offering. We really don't know why his offering was not acceptable; Scripture does not say. See Digging Deeper.)

APPLY
(10 minutes)

Option 1: Say: *When God is rebuking Cain for his attitude (Genesis 4:7), God describes sin as a thief who lurks at the door, waiting to control the person inside. Give* youth paper and pencils, and ask them to create their own simple picture of sin waiting at the door of their own life in a competitive situation. Participants may use either words or drawings.

Option 2: Give each participant a "Charting My Attitudes" handout. Explain that each line represents a graph to chart our typical behaviour in five different areas of life. Ask participants to rate themselves in each of the five areas: whether they are more like Abel, who chose excellence, or Cain. Tell participants not to complete the bottom, boxed part "Changing My Behaviour," yet.

Option: Make a graph on the floor of the meeting space with masking tape or chalk. Ask the youth to rate themselves by standing on the graph at the appropriate place, one area of life at a time. (Are there noticeable differences between the guys and girls in their attitudes about competition? If so, draw out discussion. *Some say girls are more competitive in relationships, and boys more competitive in tasks. Is this true of our group?*) Ask: *How is doing our best to please God the same or different from being competitive against other people?*

Once participants have rated where they stand in each of the five areas, ask youth to suggest a few ideas under each category of what people their age could do to improve personal attitudes.

RESPOND
(5-10 minutes)

Option 1 (after Apply, Option 1): After a few minutes of writing or drawing, post the pages on a wall and have a few participants describe what they created. Ask: *If God were to come talk to you after a time of competition, whatever form it may take, would God be pleased with how you handled yourself, or would God be disappointed?* If your group tends to share openly, have youth find a partner and discuss this question together. Then ask: *What might God want you to change about how you respond in times of competition?*

Option 2 (after Apply, Option 2): After participants have rated each of the five areas of their lives, have them complete the second part of the handout. Ask youth to choose one area of their lives to work on, then have them write down one thing they will do each day for one week, as an attempt to become more like Abel, who chose to please God in all he did.

After either option, close in prayer, thanking God that competition can motivate us to strive for excellence. Ask God to help each one of us strive for excellence in all we do this coming week, and to help us resist the temptation to let sin enter our competitions.

REFLECT AND LOOK AHEAD

It is quite possible that some in the group feel desperate for success, whether it is in friendship, academics, sports, or almost anything else. Hopefully this lesson will help your youth to examine some of their attitudes towards competition, both success and failure. Did you emphasize that, more than winning and losing, God desires us to be and do our best? In the next lesson, you will think together about how words can influence how others react in competitive situations.

DIGGING DEEPER

The story of Cain and Abel (Genesis 4:1-9)* is both fascinating and troubling. Did Cain feel competitive with Abel before the offering? Did he give up before even trying to bring an excellent offering? Did Cain feel that pleasing God wasn't important? Once his sacrifice was rejected, why did he react against his brother? These are questions left unanswered in Scripture. Both brothers had the opportunity to please God by bringing sacrifices that were of the highest standards. Yet for some reason Cain's offering, or the attitude that motivated it, was not pleasing to God.

Life has a way of forcing each of us into a place of choosing. When we find ourselves competing with someone, whether we are winners or losers, we need to choose how we will react. Will we choose to be arrogant about victory? Will we choose to be frustrated and jealous about defeat? Like both Cain and Abel, each of us has plenty of opportunities to please God by making choices that honour God and bring harmony in our daily relationships.

If Cain chooses to let sin be his master, everybody loses: Abel loses his life, Cain loses his success as a farmer (Genesis 4:12), and Adam and Eve lose both sons, one to death and the other to the land of Nod (Genesis 4:16). Allowing sin to be the master causes pain and hardship not just for the one who chooses, but for the whole community. The notion that my sin hurts no one is far from reality. The story nowhere seems to say that anger is wrong, only that Cain must choose how he will respond to that anger he feels. In the end, Cain's response to his anger alienates him from God, his brother, and the rest of his family. It is a high price to pay.

It is important to note that at no time does the story assume that Cain's future fate is sealed. After being confronted by God, Cain has a very real decision to make. Sin is waiting at his door. Will he decide to let it be his master? Cain is forced to choose between two masters, God or sin. Choosing whom you will follow is a theme found several times in the pages of Scripture (Deut. 30:19-20; Josh. 24:15; Mark 10:17-23; Luke 16:1-15). Cain's future depends on what he chooses. Even after Cain chooses to let sin be his master, to let his anger lead to murder, he is not beyond God's mercy. God punishes him, but much less severely "than law and custom might dictate" (Roop, Eugene F., *Believers Church Bible Commentary: Genesis*, Kitchener, Herald Press, 1987, p. 53).

The Cain and Abel story shows a furthering of the disharmony in creation that resulted from Adam and Eve choosing to disobey God. Cain, like his father, chose sin instead of wholehearted obedience to God. This same disharmony rears its ugly head in our competitive relationships today. Youth can know that the Bible addresses this current-day problem, and that God has solutions and mercy for our own murderous attitudes.

*Note the retelling of Genesis 4:1-24 found in the book, *The Storyteller's Companion to the Bible,* edited by Michael E. William (Nashville, Abingdon Press, 1991, pp. 45-47).

HANDOUTS
Pleasing God or Spilling Blood
Charting My Attitudes

Pleasing God
or Spilling Blood

Genesis 4:1-9 (New Century Version)

Narrator: Adam had sexual relations with his wife Eve, and she became pregnant and gave birth to Cain. Eve said,

Eve: With the Lord's help, I have given birth to a man.

Narrator: After that, Eve gave birth to Cain's brother Abel. Abel took care of flocks, and Cain became a farmer. Later, Cain brought some food from the ground as a gift to God. Abel brought the best parts from some of the firstborn of his flock. The Lord accepted Abel and his gift, but he did not accept Cain and his gift. So Cain became very angry and felt rejected. The Lord said to Cain,

God: Why are you angry? Why do you look so unhappy? If you do things well, I will accept you, but if you do not do them well, sin is ready to attack you. Sin wants you, but you must rule over it.

Narrator: Cain said to his brother Abel,

Cain: Let's go out into the field.

Narrator: While they were out in the field, Cain attacked his brother Abel and killed him. Later, the Lord said to Cain,

God: Where is your brother Abel?

Narrator: Cain answered,

Cain: I don't know. Is it my job to take care of my brother?

Narrator: Then the Lord said,

God: What have you done? Your brother's blood is crying out to me from the ground. And now you will be cursed in your work with the ground, the same ground where your brother's blood fell and where your hands killed him.

CHARTING MY ATTITUDES

Both Cain and Abel brought gifts to God. Each had the opportunity to please God. Abel chose to bring his very best, but Cain displeased God. The five lines below represent areas of life where we have opportunities to please God. In each of the five areas, decide and mark on the line where you think you stand most of the time. Do you respond more like Abel, giving your very best, or more like Cain?

1. At home I…

    …do my best to please God   …don't do my best

    <-->

2. At school I…

    …do my best to please God   …don't do my best

    <-->

3. With friends I…

    …do my best to please God   …don't do my best

    <-->

4. In sports I…

    …do my best to please God   …don't do my best

    <-->

5. At church I…

    …do my best to please God   …don't do my best

    <-->

Changing My Behaviour
Pick one of the categories above, and decide on one activity you can do every day this week to bring more excellence into your attitudes and actions. Write down what you will do here:

SESSION 2

PREPARATION

PUZZLING POPULARITY

Scripture text: 1 Samuel 18:6-16

Key verse: Saul was very angry, for this saying displeased him. He said, "They have ascribed to David ten thousands, and to me they have ascribed thousands; what more can he have but the kingdom?" So Saul eyed David from that day on. (1 Samuel 18:8-9)

Faith focus: The chant of the women, while well-meaning, brought much tension into the relationship between Saul and David. What could have been a good relationship between Saul and David turned into one characterized by hatred and jealousy.

Session goal: Help youth discover that their words can sometimes stoke the fires of unnecessary conflict and competition between people.

Materials and advance preparation needed:
- Handout, "Puzzling Popularity" (Focus, Option 1)
- "Sticks and stones…" poster (Focus, Option 2)
- Newsprint and marker (Focus, Option 2 and Connect, Option 1)
- "News Flash" handout (Hear and Enter)
- Paper and pencils (Apply, Option 2 and Respond, Option 3)
- Small stones and permanent markers (Respond, Option 1)
- "Burden Box" and matches (Respond, Option 2)

EXPLORATION

Option 1: Divide into pairs and give each pair a "Puzzling Popularity" handout and a pencil. This activity is similar to the game ***Scattegories***. Starting with the letter "P," when you call out a category (for example, professional sports, teachers, pizza companies, pets, beverages, careers) participants are to quickly think of and write down the names of companies, products, or people connected to that category in some way who could be described as popular. Allow just under a minute for each category. Call out a different category for each letter on the page. Once you

FOCUS
(5 minutes)

careers
pets
pizza companies
teachers
sports drinks
fast food restaurants
breakfast foods
medicine cabinet items
actor/actress
professional sports

have called out a category for each letter, have teams call out their answers. Determine which team had the most unique answers.

Option 2: On newsprint or chalkboard, write the phrase, "Sticks and stones may break my bones, but names will never hurt me." Ask the group to decide if this is a true statement or not, and why. Have the group list hurtful names beside the phrase that people their age use against each other.

CONNECT
(5-10 minutes)

Option 1: Stay in the same teams as in Focus, Option 1. Have pairs think of something they could say that would deflate the victor's joy. Have the groups write their sayings on a large piece of newsprint. Once all the pairs have written down their saying, ask the class how they might feel if someone said one of these things to them after they had just worked very hard to accomplish something difficult.

Option 2 (after Focus, Option 1): Have group members think of a time they said something hurtful. Without giving details, have a few students explain why they said what they did. Next ask group members to remember a time someone said something hurtful to them. Ask a few to explain how they felt. Possibly relate a story from your own experience. Ask: *Is it possible to say something nice in a hurtful way?* Have the group try to give a few examples.

Transition comment: *It's easy to speak without thinking. However, sometimes when people feel as though they have to compete for the admiration and attention of others, a poorly chosen word can be the difference between a friendship and a fight. In today's Bible story we will see how the words of a few people brought great tension into the relationship of two popular people.*

HEAR AND ENTER
(10-15 minutes)

Recruit six volunteers for a dramatic retelling of 1 Samuel 18:6-16 (or double up parts in a small group). Give these readers each a copy of the "News Flash" handout, and give them two minutes to prepare. (While the readers are preparing, tell the rest of the group to imagine that they are watching a TV show when their program is interrupted by a special news bulletin.)

After the dramatic reading, have a few volunteers describe what was happening in the story. Say: *Here is what the Bible records the crowds actually saying about King Saul and the future king, David.* Read 1 Samuel 18:7. Ask:

- *Why do you think King Saul became so angry at the crowd's song?* (He feared David would replace him as king. He liked getting praise and was jealous...)
- *How do you think David felt when he heard what the crowds were saying about him and Saul?* (good, embarrassed, fearful of Saul's reaction...)
- *Do you think the women were trying to make Saul jealous? Why or why not?*
- *Do you think we should praise people who have done something good? How or why should we be careful in doing so?*

Divide into groups of two or three, and have groups think up a new phrase, one that would be helpful for both Saul and David. After a few moments have groups share their ideas.

Option 1: Stay in small groups. Ask each group to create a case study (or choose one of the following) describing a similar situation happening in their school, church, or on one of their teams or bands. Ask groups to discuss their scenario and come up with two different endings: one, a compliment or word of praise that escalates the tension between the individuals; and the other, a compliment that is helpful and encouraging for both individuals in each situation.

Possible situations (in all cases, assume that the individuals are normally on friendly terms with each other):

1. Bob and Sheldon are both top students. Bob beats Sheldon for highest overall grade, and tension erupts between these two.
2. LeeAnn and Beth both have been asked to audition for the title role in this year's school musical. Beth gets the lead role and LeeAnn is asked to play a smaller part.
3. At church, both Dan and Stan volunteer with the midweek floor hockey club for neighborhood kids. After a few weeks it becomes apparent that the kids like Dan more than Stan.
4. Jill and Amy are friends from church who attend different schools. Each plays on their school's basketball team. Both teams end up in the city finals. Both are nervous and excited about the coming game.

APPLY
(10 minutes)

5. Senior highers Mary and David are being accepted as new members at church. Part of the process involves them sharing their faith stories with the entire church. Both are nervous, but Mary is able to give her testimony without appearing the least bit uncomfortable. David, on the other hand, has to read his testimony and even loses his place once.

Option 2: Stay in small groups. Give each paper and a pencil. Have pairs write the numbers 1 through 3 down the side of the page. Have everybody imagine a victory parade for the competitors in a major school tournament. Beside number one, have participants write a compliment that might make the second- and third-place finishers angry instead of happy. Beside number two, have everybody write a criticism that might have made the winner unhappy and the runners-up feel better about their performance. Say: *It's not that hard to come up with compliments or criticisms that make one person feel good and another person feel bad. The real challenge comes when we try to speak so that everybody ends up being encouraged.* Beside number three, have pairs create a compliment that would help both a winner and a loser feel better.

RESPOND
(5-10 minutes)

Option 1: Hand out a small stone to each participant. Ask everybody to think of one individual (someone from school, church, a sibling, or even a parent) to whom they have a hard time speaking words that are encouraging. Pass around a permanent marker and ask participants to write this person's initials on their stone. After a moment's pause for a silent prayer, ask each person to pray for the person they were thinking of. Then ask the participants to put the stone in their pocket and carry it around every day for one week. Every time they notice their stone, they are to say a brief prayer for that person.

Option 2: Ask three volunteers to close in prayer:
• one person asks God to help us see God's hand at work in all good things that happen in life;
• another person asks God to help us learn to be content with who we are, no matter what others say;
• the third person prays that God would help us to become positive influences in the relationships around us.

Option **3:** Give each participant a paper and pencil. Ask them to divide the paper in half. Ask students to write on one half the name of someone who has hurt them with what they have said. On the second half of the paper, ask youth to write an idea for how they could relate to this person in a way that promotes forgiveness. Have students think about what they can do to show this person they have forgiven them. Ask students to fold the papers in half and place them in the "Burden Box" (a shoebox with a slot on the top like a ballot box) to symbolize that they are giving these burdens (the grudges they have carried) to God. Take the box to the parking lot and carefully set it on fire. As the smoke rises, invite students to silently pray God's blessings on the persons whose names they wrote.

REFLECT AND LOOK AHEAD

Everybody wants to be accepted by those around them. Often this leads to subtle forms of competition. The Bible tells us to think not only of our own interests, but also of the interests of others (Philippians 2:4). Were you able to help your youth analyze how they respond verbally to individuals competing for popularity all around them—and perhaps how to do it better? The next lesson also looks at competition for the admiration and acceptance of others, but focuses on how this might affect family life.

DIGGING DEEPER

One of the significant issues in the story in 1 Samuel 18:6-16 is the jealousy that Saul feels for David. The crowds, in their praise of the victory over the Philistines, obviously add to Saul's frustration. This relationship soon turns nasty when Saul hears the words of the women's song and imagines that David will be the one to replace him on the throne. Without God's Spirit to guide and direct him, Saul allows his jealousy to become violent. The day after the parade, Saul attempts to kill David with a spear.

Ronald F. Youngblood observes that the refrain sung by the women (18:7) containing the phrase, "thousands... ten thousands," is a common Old Testament parallel which simply indicates a large number, not necessarily ascribing greater worth to one or the other (*Expositor's Bible Commentary*, ed. Frank E. Gaebelein, 1992, Zondervan Publishing House, Grand Rapids, p. 708). This song may simply be giving equal praise to both Saul and David, yet Saul chooses to interpret it as a slight against himself. Imagine how differently the story would have turned out if Saul had immediately repented of his jealous attitude and humbly accepted the words of the women as a shout of victory for all Israel, not just for Saul and David.

The song of the women is very much like a double-edged sword. It is intended to praise this incredible, miraculous victory over the Philistines, yet at the same time somehow causes more trouble than good. Imagine how differently the story would have turned out if the women had praised God, instead of these two leaders, for the victory.

While the story of Saul, David, and the women is from a time and place that we can hardly imagine, the situation is not entirely foreign. Every day, people compete with each other for respect, admiration, and acceptance. It is in these common situations that a wisely chosen word can mean the difference between strengthened and encouraged individuals or the destruction of meaningful relationships. Jealousy, competition, and encouraging words are timeless realities.

Proverbs 27:4 points to the power of jealousy: "Wrath is cruel, anger is overwhelming, but who is able to stand before jealousy?" Virtually every account of jealousy in the Bible ends up with the destruction of relationships, sometimes even with the loss of life. In Luke 15, Jesus tells the story of the prodigal son. In contrast to the innocent but harmful words of the women's song about Saul and David, the father's words to the jealous older son promote healing of the relationship, not further destruction of it.

When people begin to feel their worth threatened by others, even the most innocent of praises can turn once-friendly relationships into harmful competitions. Scripture encourages us to choose our words carefully, "Let no evil talk come out of your mouths, but only what is useful for building up, as there is need, so that your words may give grace to those who hear" (Eph. 4:29). Does this mean that we should not praise people for a job well done, or a special attribute? Not necessarily. Perhaps it does point out that we need to be more sensitive to the existence of competition, and be ready to minister words of encouragement and grace to all those involved. Ultimately, relationships are bolstered when we together acknowledge God as the originator of all good accomplishments. Teens can learn early of the importance of such words.

HANDOUTS
Puzzling Popularity
News Flash

PUZZLING POPULARITY

Your leader will call out several categories, a different one for each letter of the word, "POPULAR." Your task is to write down the most unique names you can think of for each category your leader calls out. The trick, however, is that the names you put down must start with the same letter that the rest of the group is working on. For example, when your leader calls out the category "religious figures," you might write down under the letter "P" "Pope Pious X" as one of your answers. Be creative; points are only awarded for unique answers.

P   O   P   O   P   U   L   A   R

NEWS*FLASH*

Newscaster: We interrupt our regularly scheduled program to bring you this special news flash. The long-standing war between Israel and the Philistines took an amazing turn this afternoon. After an agonizing 40-day standoff, the Philistine giant Goliath was defeated by a 14-year-old boy from a small town called Bethlehem. Apparently this young boy arrived at the battle lines simply to bring a care package to his older brothers, who are soldiers in the king's army. When the boy discovered that the entire Israelite army was afraid to fight this giant, he went out himself with only a slingshot and faith in God as his weapons. Amazingly, he defeated the giant with one incredible stone.

We take you now to reporter Bob in Jerusalem where the victory parade is in progress.

Reporter Bob: The atmosphere here today is absolutely electric. When King Saul and the army marched into the city, the crowds cheered the victory. But when this boy wonder, David, came in, the crowd went positively crazy. Here's what people had to say:

Person 1: Wow! We thought that Saul was a great king, but this David, he's incredible...

Person 2: If only David was the king. He is just what this country needs—someone brave, courageous, and decisive...

Person 3: Ooh, that David. He sure is something. I bet old King Saul could learn a thing or two from him. Does anyone know what his phone number is?

Reporter Bob: Excuse me, Ma'am, telephones won't be invented for a few thousand years yet. But enough about that, here comes the king. Let's see what he has to say...

King Saul: Can you believe what these crowds are saying? One little victory and suddenly this David is so much greater than I am!?

Newscaster: There you have it, folks, military victory for Israel and political turmoil for King Saul.

SESSION 3
PREPARATION

Scripture text: Genesis 27, 32–33

Key verse: Now Esau hated Jacob because of the blessing with which his father had blessed him, and Esau said to himself, "The days of mourning for my father are approaching; then I will kill my brother Jacob." (Genesis 27:41)

Faith focus: Jacob and his mother plotted to get Isaac's blessing for Jacob, instead of for Esau, to whom it was rightly entitled. Despite the anger, hatred, and betrayal, the brothers eventually forgave each other and reestablished their relationship.

Session goal: Help youth understand that when competition occurs at home, the results can be extremely painful. When this is the case, God provides a way, through forgiveness and reconciliation, for real hope and healing to occur.

WHEN HOME IS HARD

Materials and advance preparation needed:
- Magazines, newspapers, glue, tape, markers, large piece of paper (Focus, Option 3)
- Pencils, tape, large paper (Connect, Option 1)
- Give handout, "The Geraldo Ricky Jesse Show," to two volunteers to play the roles of host and guest (Hear and Enter)
- Paper and pencils (Apply, Option 2)

EXPLORATION

Option 1: Divide into pairs. Instruct each person to put on their best scowl. Now compete to see who can stare at their partner the longest without losing the scowl. Compete until you establish the one or two most enduring scowls. Ask: *When was the last time you felt like scowling for real?* (If the youth don't offer them, draw out examples of family tensions.)

Option 2: Have pairs sit back-to-back on the floor. On "Go!" have partners begin to gently push

FOCUS
(5 minutes)

against each other. Every three or four seconds instruct the pairs to increase the pressure. Do this for a few minutes, then switch partners and try again.

Option 3: Have participants cut out pictures from magazines, stories from newspapers, or create their own pictures or phrases that describe frustrating family experiences. Glue all of these onto one large piece of paper under the heading "When Home is Hard."

CONNECT
(5-10 minutes)

Option 1: Say: *Sometimes families can act and feel much like a "scowl-down." Even in our families—as different as they may be—we become unhappy because we compete with each other for love, respect, and attention.*

Trace the outline of a student onto a large sheet of paper. Name this picture "Jake." Hang Jake on the wall or door. Ask youth to write one- or two-word ideas of ways that families compete with each other (see list of possibilities below). After there are a number of ideas written on Jake, say something like: *Family competition and conflict can end up leaving scars and stains that we could wear for life. The various ways we compete in our families often does more to tear us down than it does to build us up.*

Have participants carefully tear off a word or phrase from Jake, and tape it onto their arm like an armband to wear for the rest of the class.

Option 2 (after Focus, Option 2): Say: *Sometimes people in families compete with each other for love, attention, respect, or admiration. This can be a lot like pushing against each other as we just did.* Ask participants to brainstorm a list of ways that people in families compete with each other.

Some possibilities:
- One child gets a later curfew than another sibling had at the same age. Or, household rules in general seem more flexible for one child in the family than for the other kids.
- Parents hassle one child more than another about school performance.
- One child is Mom's favorite, another appears to be Dad's favorite, and a third might feel totally alone in the family.
- Two kids compete for the parents' attention, one by doing well in school and sports, the other by acting out.
- One child is often compared to a very talented older sibling.

- Mom and Dad don't get along well, and seem to be competing for the love of their kids.
- Dad is often seen taking the side of one child, but rarely the side of the others.
- When two siblings fight, Mom takes the side of one; Dad takes the side of the other.

Option 3 (after Focus, Option 3): Divide into pairs. Have pairs guess what percentage of the time young people their age get along with their mothers. Next have pairs guess the same thing for youth and their fathers. Last, have pairs answer the same question for youth and their siblings. Have participants write these guesses somewhere on the collage.

Transition comment: *It would be nice if every home was a safe haven from the pressures and competition of everyday life. But unfortunately, that isn't always the case. Our families are all different; and every family has troubles. The story of Jacob and Esau from the book of Genesis is a perfect example of a family allowing competition at home to get out of control.*

HEAR AND ENTER
(15 minutes)

Recruit two volunteers ahead of time: one to play the role of a talk show host (preferably one of the class members), and an adult to play the role of Esau.

Set up one corner of your meeting space like a talk show, complete with nice chairs, coffee table, and even a couple of soft drinks on the table. Say: *The Scripture text today is from Genesis 27, 32, and 33. Instead of reading the text, why don't we listen in as a world-famous talk show host interviews one of the main characters from the story in Genesis* (see handout: "The Geraldo Ricky Jesse Show").

Dim the lights and shine a spotlight, if possible, as the world-famous talk show host enters the room.

After the talk show is complete, divide into groups of three or four. Say: *Both Jacob and Esau seemed to want the same thing. What was it?* (the blessing) *Are there other reasons you can imagine for the conflict between the two brothers? In your groups, come up with three practical ideas for how Esau's family could have gotten along better.* Reconvene the group and share ideas.

APPLY
(10 minutes)

Option 1: Say: *The father's blessing was a sign of respect, admiration, and trust. What kinds of things do young people today do to try to earn the love, attention,* *and respect that they need and want at home? (If you have time, talk about loss of trust—how it happens and how it may contribute to family tensions.)*

Option 2: Say: *Esau and his dad had a lot in common: Both seemed to like the same kinds of things. Jacob and his mother also seemed to have a special relationship.* Divide into four groups. Have each group write a brief letter to either the father, the mother, Esau, or Jacob. The letters could suggest things this person could do to bring more harmony and less competition into family life. Share the letters with the group.

RESPOND
(10 minutes)

Option 1 (for use with Connect, Option 1): Say: *Jacob and Esau eventually patched up their highly competitive relationship. Let's see if we can patch up our friend Jake. On the back of the papers you have taped to your arms, write a positive alternative to the competition listed earlier. Tape Jake back together as completely as possible.* Comment that Jake will look a little scarred. Tell youth that God can completely put him back together, just as is possible when we are hurt by family rivalries.

Option 2: Ask group members to think of their own families, or of friends who seem to be in competition with family members. Close by asking youth to pray silently for their family or friend. Ask youth also to pray every day this next week for that same need. After a few moments of silence, close in prayer for the whole group something like: *Dear God, just as you brought forgiveness, reconciliation, and friendship back to Jacob and Esau, please help us find these in our own families. Help us live as friends instead of as competitors at home. Amen.*

Option 3: Ask students to each pick an issue from the life of Jacob and Esau that is present in their lives. Ask students to join you in closing prayer. Have students complete the following prayer: *Dear God, please help me turn* (negative characteristic) *into* (positive characteristic), *so that peace and joy may be found in my family.*

REFLECT AND LOOK AHEAD

Family life can be terribly difficult at times. Be aware that this lesson may have raised uncomfortable feelings and difficult questions in some of your youth. Be available to talk with any youth outside of class who may be struggling in difficult family situations.

Look early in the week at the next session plan. Let it "simmer" as you conduct your other activities the next few days.

DIGGING DEEPER

The story of Jacob and Esau is part of the ongoing saga of God establishing a nation from the promise made to Abraham and Sarah. It is a story filled with twists and turns, great sacrifice and, at times, even greater betrayal. The *Believers Bible Commentary* on Genesis provides some helpful insights about these tumultuous relationships.

As the older of the two, Esau had a clear right to his father's blessing. When he lost the blessing through the deception of Jacob and Rebekah, Esau was understandably crushed. It seems strange to us today that Isaac was unable to undo the obvious wrong, and return the blessing to Esau.

Before the twins were born, God promised Rebekah that the older would serve the younger. If God made a strange promise like this, surely God could make it happen. The story sounds as though both Rebekah and Jacob thought they needed to help God make this promise come true. So they resorted to cruelty, deception, and malice towards Esau. Surely these two would have known from their family history that God doesn't need human effort to make his promises come true. Abraham and Sarah were childless until God stepped in (Genesis 20:17–21:2). Even Rebekah was unable to have children until Isaac prayed, and God answered (25:21).

As we read of the deception of Isaac by Jacob and Rebekah, we need to remember the strange bargain that Jacob and Esau had made earlier in their lives. Esau returned from an unsuccessful hunting trip weak and starving. Instead of simply offering his brother some food, Jacob forced Esau to give up his claim on his rights as the firstborn son. Esau agreed because he seemed to think he would die if Jacob didn't give him food immediately. Esau gave in too easily, showing how little he cared about being the firstborn son. It seems that even though God had chosen the younger son, this choice didn't violate the interests of either Esau or Jacob. Why didn't Jacob simply then go to his father bearing God's promise to Rebekah and Esau's promise to Jacob, and ask Isaac for the blessing? Was God honored by the deception?

While the story of Jacob and Esau covers much time and territory, it does leave out some important details. The story never does indicate how Esau was able to harness his hatred for Jacob, and turn it into friendship and hospitality. God obviously did a major work in his life. Spend some time thinking for yourself about the kinds of things that might have helped Esau turn around. This time of meditation will help you lead your group's thinking during the session.

HANDOUT:
The Geraldo Ricky Jesse Show

The Geraldo Ricky Jesse Show

(based on Genesis 27, 32–33 *New Century Version*)

Host: Ladies and gentlemen, our special guest today once threatened to kill his own twin brother. Let's have a big round of applause for the big hairy guy himself... ESAU!
(Esau walks in and sits down, looking a little shy.)

Host: Esau, you've gained considerable fame as the man who made it into the Bible because you threatened to kill your twin brother. Everyone thought he was a goner, but instead you chose to forgive him. Tell us, what made you so angry in the first place?

Esau: As you know, Geraldo, when I was a young man, a dad passed on his blessing to his oldest son just before he died. This is a really big deal because along with the blessing comes the biggest part of the inheritance, and the right to make major family decisions. Jacob—my younger brother—and I competed for years for the love and attention of our parents. I was my dad's favourite, and Jacob was always Momma's little helper. You know how it is, Ricky...

Host: Sorry, Esau, I'm just a TV character, so… no, I don't know how it is. But for the sake of good ratings, let's say I do.

Esau: Uh, okay, Jesse, let me get back to the story... Well, Dad was really old. He was blind and hard of hearing. He couldn't chew too well, but he still loved a good barbecued steak. When the time came for me to receive my father's blessing, Dad asked me to go out and hunt for him one last time. While I was gone, my mother and Jake tricked Dad into thinking Jake was me. Dad gave his blessing to Jacob. I was furious when I found out.

Host: But, Esau, couldn't you just tell your dad that it was all a mistake?

Esau: Actually, when I told Dad what happened, he said the blessing couldn't be undone—even though Mom and Jake had cheated to get it.

Host: So what happened?

Esau: That's when I said the words I'll always regret: "My father will soon die, and I will be sad for him. Then I will kill Jacob."

Host: So you were planning to make it a double funeral. How devious!

Esau: That's right, except Mom warned Jake and he ran away. I let him go. He'd die out there in the wilderness in a few days anyway, so why waste my energy chasing him down?

Host: Which brings us to the incredible conclusion to your story. Instead of killing your brother, you chose to forgive him instead. What changed your mind?

Esau: I heard that Jake didn't die like I was hoping. Talk about being bitter. Forgiving him took me several years. Over time God showed me that living with hatred and bitterness was harder than forgiving. So when Jake showed up years later, in need of help, I knew what I had to do.

Host: You got a lawyer and sued him?

Esau: No, I put the past behind me and let God help me forgive.

Host: Well, there you have it, ladies and gentlemen, the incredible story of a normal, everyday guy who discovered the freedom of forgiveness. *(Calls for applause)* And let's give an even bigger round of applause to me, your incredible host. *(Applause)*

SESSION 4

PREPARATION

Scripture text: Luke 22:24-30

Key verse: The greatest among you must become like the youngest, and the leader like one who serves. (Luke 22:26*b*)

Faith focus: After Jesus taught his disciples about the coming kingdom of God, they began to compete for positions of honour and power. Jesus responded by explaining that in God's kingdom the ones who serve will be honored by God as worthy of greater responsibility, and will be blessed.

Session goal: Help youth understand that real joy comes not from competing for power, position, or popularity, but from serving God and others.

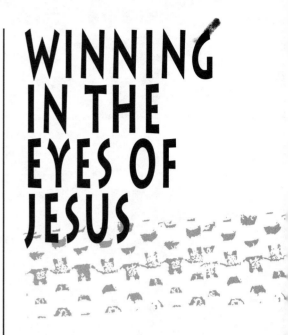

WINNING IN THE EYES OF JESUS

Materials and advance preparation needed:
- Newspapers (Focus, Option 1)
- Magazines, newspapers, poster board, flyers, glue, scissors (Focus, Option 2)
- Newsprint and markers (Connect, Option 1)
- Paper and pencils (Connect, Option 2 and Hear and Enter)
- Bibles (Hear and Enter)
- Markers and several posters (Apply, Option 1)
- Two signs: "Happy to Serve" and "Happy to Be Served" (Apply, Option 2)
- Newsprint and marker (Apply, Option 3)
- "Seven-Day Servant" handout (Respond, Option 2)

EXPLORATION

Option 1: Divide into coed pairs to compete for the title "Rulers of the Heap." Give each pair roughly the same amount of newspaper. Race to build the tallest heap of paper, using the paper. At the end of three minutes the participants with the tallest heap of paper are declared the "Rulers of the Heap." There are only two rules to this competition: (1) Only paper is permitted as a material for building the heaps, and

FOCUS
(5-10 minutes)

(2) No group may destroy another group's work. (It might be a good idea to **hint** that there is a sure-fire way to build a tall heap under the rules given. Do not actually say, though, that by working together, sharing their newspapers among groups, they can win.)

Option 2: Hand out poster board, newspapers, flyers, glue, scissors, and magazines. Divide youth into two groups. Ask the first group to create a collage of words, phrases, and images that communicate that it is better to receive and be looked up to than it is to give and serve. Ask group number two to create a collage based on the opposite message, that it is better to give than to receive. After a few minutes have groups share what they created. Ask participants which message they think is more common in the world around them.

CONNECT
(5 minutes)

Option 1 (after Focus, Option 1): After a few minutes of building newspaper heaps, see if any groups decided to build a heap together. Have the entire group work together to build one great big heap of paper. Make two columns on a large piece of newsprint. Say: *When we worked together we created something huge. Why do you think people don't work together more often?* Record their ideas on the first column. On the second column, record group suggestions for possible benefits of helping others (sharing resources and possessions, swapping talents, and so on).

Option 2: Hand out paper and pencils to each youth. Say: *People do all sorts of things to become great in the eyes of others. See if you can imagine how the people I'm going to list for you prepare to earn the admiration of others.* Present several types of people and have each participant list ideas about what each might do to become great. Examples:
1. a hall-of-fame hockey player
2. the most-sought-after mechanic in town
3. an incredible friend
4. Teacher of the Year
5. a Nobel Peace Prize winner
6. an award-winning musician
7. a Christian teenager

Ask: *How do you imagine competition affects what these people do/did to achieve their status?* (Elicit answers that are both positive and negative.) *Do you suppose they might have hurt someone to get where they are? How?*

Transition comment: *People often compete, hoping to win so that they will receive the admiration of those around them. It is a common idea that if you want to be really happy you need to forget about the needs of others and look out for yourself. Even Jesus' disciples acted this way sometimes.*

HEAR AND ENTER
(15 minutes)

Divide into groups of four or five. Have each group create a quiz consisting of seven questions based on Luke 22:24-30. The quizzes should include both observation questions (what is happening), and interpretation (what does it mean) questions. Have groups close their Bibles and exchange quizzes. Give groups three minutes to complete the other's quizzes.

At the end of three minutes, have groups share both their quizzes and their answers with the rest of the group. After hearing the various questions and answers, ask the groups to summarize the main point of the passage in one sentence.

Say: *Competition in the world around us is often about trying to be number one. Jesus helps his followers understand that, in God's kingdom, the one who challenges this me-first competition by serving others is the one who receives the greatest prize—the honour that only God can give.*

APPLY
(5 minutes)

Option 1: Say: *Jesus washed people's feet, spent time with social outcasts, and healed and listened when he was tired and hungry.* Point out several posters you have hung at various places around the meeting space with the title "Imitating Jesus." On each poster is written a setting (such as: at home, at school, Christmas shopping, when two friends are fighting, getting short-changed at a store, finding out a friend has trouble at home, watching an elderly neighbour struggle with yard work, meeting a scary stranger). Divide into small groups, give each group a marker, direct each to a poster, and ask groups to brainstorm things people their age could do to follow Jesus' example and serve others. After two minutes have groups move to another poster and continue brainstorming.

After a few minutes of brainstorming, say: *Jesus repeatedly asked his disciples to be humble, to put others first, to serve others. Why do you think the disciples had a hard time actually doing this?*

Option 2: Post two signs on opposite walls of the meeting space, one saying "Happy to Serve" and the other saying "Happy to Be Served." Ask participants to place themselves somewhere between these two signs depending on which phrase describes them better under the following circumstances:

1. Cleaning day at home
2. At school after a long day of classes
3. An elderly neighbour needs some unpleasant yard work done
4. Three hungry people and only two pieces of pizza
5. A water main breaks and floods your school. Volunteers are needed to help clean up.
6. A young man with two small children enters a very crowded bus where you happen to have a seat.
7. The fence needs painting and a group of friends has invited you to join them at the beach for the day.

After these seven statements, ask the class why some people would rather be served than serve others. *What is wrong with wanting to be served, with wanting positions of honour? When is it okay to be the recipient—to be served?*

Option 3: Ask youth to think of the kindest, most helpful person they know. Have participants call out things they really like about these people. Record their ideas on a large piece of newsprint.

Say: *People who do not know God often compete to be the most important, the most popular, the smartest, the strongest, the richest, the best. Why might it be wrong to want to be number one?* Divide into groups of three to discuss this question for two minutes. Have groups share their ideas. (Possible answers: Wanting to be better than others can lead to hurting others in the process; to hurting ourselves by damaging our health, reputation, relationship with God; to valuing the wrong things above what is really important...) Next, tell the groups: *Jesus told his followers that instead of primarily looking out for themselves, they should look out for others.* Ask groups to discuss why it might have been hard for the disciples to do this. After a few moments, again have groups share their ideas, then ask the entire group: *Why would anyone want to do what Jesus is asking?* Finally, ask groups to imagine that someone their age decided to do exactly what Jesus is asking. *What kinds of things would they do?*

RESPOND
(5 minutes)

Summarize the lesson by saying: *Competition with others is a normal part of our lives. Not so in God's kingdom, at least not in the traditional sense. As followers of Jesus we resist the constant competition we face by learning to serve others in the name of Jesus. Becoming like this requires time, practice, inner transformation, and a community of friends who can assist us in this task.*

Option 1 (after Apply, Option 1): Ask participants to wander around the room and look at all the ideas written on the posters of things people their age could do to follow Jesus' example and serve others. Ask individuals to pick one idea from the "at home" and "at school" lists that they will try to put into practice the coming week. Ask each youth to tell the group what they will do. Close in prayer, asking God to help the youth discover the joy that comes from serving others.

Option 2: Give each participant a "Seven-Day Servant" handout. Have them choose one act of service for each of the next seven days. Explain that the act of service must be anonymous if possible, and must cost them something—time, money, pride, or energy. Have youth keep a record of the service they do each day. Ask them to bring the handouts back with them for the next session.

Option 3: As a group, plan together to do a small service project. Be creative, realistic, and plan to spend about two hours working at something together that primarily benefits others. (When the group gets together to actually do the experience, spend a few minutes in prayer for the people who will be helped. Talk afterwards together about the experience: what was good about it, what was hard, if they would do it again, what they would change about the experience. If it was fun or emotionally rewarding, was it true service? Why, or why not? If it was not fun, will it be rewarded? How? When?)

Following are a few service opportunity ideas that can be a lot of fun:
- On a hot summer day, fill a large cooler with ice and canned drinks. Go to a local park and hand out the drinks to everyone you meet.
- During Christmas shopping season, buy several dozen roses, go to a local mall and look for people to give them to: harried moms, overworked cashiers, Salvation Army volunteers.
- Rake-and-Run: Pick a neighbourhood near the church during the fall and go door-to-door in groups offering to rake people's lawns for free OR Shovel and Go: Same as the leaf raking but done during the winter after a snowfall. Possibly ask

church members to suggest names of people to go to who might particularly need these services.

- Contact a local food bank and find out if there is one particular food you could collect (such as peanut butter, rice, cereal). Challenge another youth group to see which can raise the most peanut butter in one weekend. Join together to bring the food to the food bank.
- Hold a pantry raid on a Friday night to collect food for a local gospel mission. Run the event like a scavenger hunt or car rally. Divide into teams and give each team a church address list and a time limit. Warn the church or community ahead of time that teams of youth will be coming around on a certain night asking for food. Tell why. At the end of the hunt either go to the mission as a group to deliver the food, or have a representative from the mission come speak to your group and briefly explain the work of the mission.
- Build care packages for students and missionaries living away from home. Spend the evening either shopping at a local grocery for items, or baking cookies. Include a note or card in each package and mail them immediately.
- Hold a board games night at a local seniors' home. Contact a representative from the home to set up details. Show up, make introductions, and then play some games.

REFLECT AND LOOK AHEAD

Did your youth catch the vision that becoming a servant requires, time, practice, inner transformation, and a community of friends? In a way, the session goal (understanding that real joy comes not from competing for power, position, or popularity, but from serving God and others) cannot be realized until youth actually begin to serve. *You* cannot give them the joy of service, or even explain it to them; they must experience it as a gift from God. Next lesson will further tackle the question of how we, as followers of Jesus, can learn to work together instead of against each other.

DIGGING DEEPER

The kind of kingdom Jesus was describing was completely unlike anything his disciples could imagine. Even after spending the better part of three years walking with Jesus, watching him, listening to him, learning from him, they still argued about who was the greatest, who should have the seat of honour, and who had the greatest power and position. Is it any wonder that many Christians today have trouble living lives of service and sacrifice? The disciples remind us that breaking free from the tyranny of competing for the honour of our peers or leaders is no small task.

It seems that after Jesus and the disciples had shared this last meal together, some began to argue about which of them was the greatest. Perhaps they were reflecting on who got to sit closest to Jesus at the banquet table. When Jesus and his disciples came together to share the Passover meal, we assume that the setting was typical of most banquets of the time. The table would likely not have been one long table as we often imagine, but would probably have been set up like a square with one side left open. The host would sit at the top of the square, or in the center, and all others would sit around him according to importance and rank. The most important would have sat closest to the host on the right and the next important would be placed directly to the left of the host, and so on around the table. Farthest away from the host would be those of the least social importance (William Barclay, *The Gospel of Luke*, Philadelphia, The Westminster Press, revised 1975, p. 267).

They were arguing about the exact thing Jesus had gone to great lengths to show was unimportant. Did they forget what Jesus had said when, earlier in his ministry, he had been invited to a banquet at the home of a leading Pharisee? Jesus noticed people claiming the best seats, so he said to them, "When you are invited by someone to a wedding banquet, do not sit down at the place of honour, in case someone more distinguished than you has been invited by your host." Jesus concluded this teachable moment by saying, "For all who exalt themselves will be humbled and all who humble themselves will be exalted" (Luke 14:1-11). In these words he is reminding people that God's kingdom operates by a different set of standards. Perhaps the followers also forgot the time Jesus was asked, "Who is the greatest in the kingdom of heaven?" (Matt. 18:1). Jesus replied that the greatest in the kingdom of heaven is the one who "becomes humble like this child" (18:4).

The account of the Passover meal in the Gospel of John has Jesus acting exactly like a servant when he gets out a bowl and towel, and proceeds to wash the feet of his disciples (John 13:1-17). Jesus explains to them that they are to follow his example. Jesus is illustrating by his actions, both here and in all the rest of his public ministry, that those who are a part of God's kingdom will not strive to look great, but will *be great* by serving others. He concludes by saying: "If you know these things, you are blessed if you do them" (John 13:17). Perhaps the disciples, like us, had heard these things but had not yet learned to live them out, and so discover the happiness Jesus was talking about.

Jesus came to serve, not be served, and he calls his followers to do likewise. Not just because it is the right thing to do, but because in other-centered living is true joy, not the shallow and quickly-passing joy that comes from being popular among our peers. Serving others is a way of life that must be learned. It took the disciples time to learn that, in God's kingdom, things are done differently than they are in the rest of the world. Christ came to set people free (John 8:31), free from the slavery to sin and self. Part of this freedom is the transformation of the desire to be great in the eyes of others.

Manford Gutzke says this about the kind of servant leadership that Jesus was describing: "The nice thing about it is that there is so little competition when it comes to service. There are so many opportunities. Everyone is willing to let the other person do it. A wise person will just go ahead and do it. And all the time he is doing for others, the humble soul is drawing nearer and nearer to Him who came to give Himself in service" (Gutzke, *Plain Talk on Luke*, Grand Rapids, Zondervan Publishing Company, 1966, pp. 157-158).

HANDOUT
Seven-Day Servant

Seven-Day Servant

Imagine that you're in a competition where the greatest servant at the end of the week ends up with a great prize. Pick one act of service for each day of the week, as well as a recipient. As you complete each day's chosen service, record briefly what that act cost you (time, money, pride, energy).

Day	Service	Recipient	Cost
Monday			
Tuesday			
Wednesday			
Thursday			
Friday			
Saturday			
Sunday			

SESSION 5
PREPARATION

Scripture texts: Ecclesiastes 4:9-12, Ephesians 3:16-21

Key verse: A threefold cord is not quickly broken. (Eccl. 4:12*b*)

Faith focus: God's Word emphasizes that true strength and power are gained through cooperation in striving for a common goal: being the most godlike people we can be.

Session goal: As an alternative to the negative aspects of competition, help youth discover the power of working together to become more like Jesus.

Materials and advance preparation needed:
- Paper and pencils (Focus, Option 1)
- "Adventure Together" handout, pencils (Focus, Option 2)
- 2 x 6 boards about eight feet long, one board for every eight people (Focus, Option 3)
- String, enough for four strands for each participant; newsprint/marker or chalkboard/chalk (Hear and Enter)
- Pencils, markers, paper (Apply, Option 1 and Respond, Option 1)
- String (Respond, Option 3)
- Bibles (Respond)

EXPLORATION

FOCUS
(8-12 minutes)

If you chose the "Seven-Day Servant" option last time, ask for sharing about what service youth engaged in, what it cost them, whether they received the gift of joy from God, and how.

Option 1: Ask if any youth have seen an adventure race on TV or know someone who has competed in one. Describe some of the events found in multi-day adventure races (kayaking, mountain biking, rappelling, climbing, running, orienteering, white-water rafting).

Pass out paper and pencils. Divide into teams (of five,

if your group is large enough) and ask each team to create the ultimate five-day, five-event adventure race (either using some of the events listed above, or creating their own unique events). After a few minutes have teams share their adventure race ideas with the rest of the group.

Say: *In adventure racing, teams need to work together—not just to win, but for safety and survival as well. If one part of the team struggles, the whole team struggles. For a team to win, they must learn to work together through all kinds of experiences and challenges.*

Option 2 (for groups of six or larger): Head outside to an open area (or go to a large room if the weather is cold). Ask every person to remove one shoe and place it on a pile with all of the other shoes. Divide this large pile into four smaller piles (if less than 12 youth, form two piles). Place one copy of the "Adventure Together" handout and a pencil on each pile. Explain that each pile represents a team. Each team is a unit that needs to work together. Tell them to find their shoe, join that team, read the instructions, and begin.

Option 3 (for groups of 16 or larger): Bring in several 2 x 6 boards about eight feet long. (Borrow them if possible; size does not have to be exact. If 2 x 6's are unavailable, use benches, old telephone books, tightropes, or any other item that will hold the entire team slightly above the ground.) Place these boards on the floor of your meeting space. Divide into coed teams of about eight. Have each team line up on one board in any order. Once teams are on their boards, no one may step off the boards onto the floor. Instruct teams to work together in silence. Give teams several challenges: (1) Arrange themselves according to height. (2) Arrange themselves from oldest to youngest. (3) Arrange themselves alphabetically (do not specify first or last names). Remind the groups to work in silence. After every group completes the challenge, congratulate everybody and hand out prizes for working together.

CONNECT
(5-10 minutes)

Option 1: Say: *There's an old cliché that says, "It's not whether you win or lose, it's how you play the game."* If you agree, move to my left; if you disagree, move to my right; if you are unsure or want to modify the statement, stand in the middle of the room. After each youth has chosen where to stand, ask one or two in each position to say why they agree, disagree, or are unsure.

Option 2 (after Focus, Option 2): Have each team think of a real team sport (such as basketball, football, or soccer). Now have teams briefly discuss what might happen during a game if each person on the team decided to do whatever he or she wanted, instead of working together. *Would the team win its game? Would the athletes be happy or frustrated at the end of the game? How would the coach feel?* Gather together as one large group again and ask if anyone has ever experienced something like this, where one person decided to do his or her own thing instead of working with the team. Possibly have one or two youth share a brief story about such an experience.

Option: Ask youth to share about times when they have been required to work with someone on a class project, a job at home, or similar task. *What problems arose, if any? How did they cope?*

Option 3: After groups have successfully completed the challenges on the 2 x 6 board, ask participants to describe what made the tasks possible (working together). *Imagine if one of the people on your team had decided not to cooperate. How would this have affected your ability to complete the challenges?* Have each group get back onto their 2 x 6 boards. Assign one person in each group to resist the group and do his or her own thing. Once all groups are on their boards, ask groups to line up according to shoe size, and then sit down. Ask which was easier, when everybody cooperated or when some people did their own thing. Ask: *Why don't people help each other out in everyday life more?*

Transition comment: *Team sports can be exciting, dynamic, stressful, and demanding. They require that team members work together in cooperation with each other, not in competition. In many athletic activities, the most fun comes from working together to make the team operate smoothly against the challenge of the game itself. Beating the other team becomes less important than being the best team you can be. Living as a follower of Jesus is very much like the adventure of participating in a team sport. In fact, it is the* ultimate *adventure.*

Have a volunteer read Ecclesiastes 4:9-12. Ask the class to call out ways that this passage says that two people can help each other (more work done, helping each other up, warmth, defence). Record these ideas on

HEAR AND ENTER
(10 minutes)

a newsprint or chalkboard. Have the group list ways they might have observed two people helping each other in life recently (friendship, traveling together, listening to each other, sharing meals if someone forgets a lunch...).

Hand out one strand of cotton string or thread to each participant. Ask them to try to break the string. Next, hand out three strings to each person and ask participants to braid them together. Now ask the youth to again try to break the string. Say: *It is much harder the second time because the strings give each other strength. While many of the messages in life tell us to look out for ourselves first, Ecclesiastes 4:9-12 says that real strength and help come when people choose to work together instead of competing against each other. Working together the same way these three strings do, instead of competing against each other, is an important part of following Jesus. But it may not always be entirely comfortable. It takes patience, genuine caring, vulnerability, and a desire to grow.* Spend a few moments drawing out discussion about why working together and accountability are good things, even though at times they can be hard.

APPLY
(10 minutes)

Option 1: Give each youth two pieces of paper and a pencil or colored markers, and ask them to draw two stick figure pictures. Picture one is a possible advantage that comes when two people cooperate. Picture two is one of the possible difficulties that people might encounter when trying to cooperate. After a few minutes of drawing, ask participants to display their pictures, and describe what they drew and why.

Option 2: Divide into groups of three or four and have each group create a skit that illustrates the main idea of Ecclesiastes 4:9-12, that real strength and help are found when people work together instead of against each other. Give each group about four minutes to prepare a 37-second skit. Some skit ideas:
1. Mary is concerned about a World Vision child she saw on TV, but cannot afford to sponsor the child all by herself.
2. Biff has been asked by an elderly friend of his parents to help put up storm windows. The job is big and Biff is small.
3. Donna, Dave, and Dianne each babysit on Tuesday evenings so that the kids' parents can volunteer at a food shelter. But the next day each of these three teenagers is exhausted because the kids are such a handful.

4. The church caretaker just broke his leg and cannot mow the church lawn all summer. Barry suggests that his youth group take on the task.
5. Betty is concerned about a local family that just lost their home to a fire. She wonders what can be done to help.

Option 1: Ask each youth to silently complete the following statement for themselves: "One area of my Christian faith where I could use some help from another person is..." After participants have answered this question, ask the group to form a circle. Have everybody write their name on a small piece of paper and pass it three people to the left. When everyone has received a name, ask youth to pray silently for a moment for that person. Close the time praying for the entire group, asking God to help us resist our tendencies to compete with each other and instead find our strength in cooperation. Have participants take their papers home and pray for each other all week long.

Option 2: As this series draws to a close, a good idea might be to form prayer partnerships. These partners commit to praying for each other every day for one month and to asking each other once a week how things are going and if there are any specific prayer requests. This kind of initiative would be greatly strengthened if you shared some of your own experiences of growing in faith as a result of someone's prayer and regular interest in the growth and practice of faith.

Option 3: Hand out three lengths of string (about 10 inches long each) to each youth and ask them to braid them together. Say: *These strands can remind us that we are stronger when we cooperate than we can be when we compete. Tie the ends together to make a bracelet or necklace to wear this week to remind you to cooperate rather than unnecessarily compete.*
Distribute Bibles. Close the unit by creating a reading of Ephesians 3:16-20. *This passage emphasizes that true strength comes to people from dwelling in Christ's love together as the church, not from competing for power or position.* Some ideas are:
• Have girls and boys read alternate verses.
• Create an amplified version from combining translations.
• Ask one or two participants to pantomime vari-

ous elements of the verses as they are reading (bow, heart, breadth and length and height…).

Dismiss the youth with the challenge to live out cooperation and love in the competitive situations of their lives: *We have learned the past weeks that an alternative way of life is possible for followers of Jesus—not only possible, but life-giving, affirming, challenging, and rewarding. Remember to continue to look for opportunities to serve others and work together, even in the midst of competitions. It is a way of life that takes practice and commitment, but once the journey is begun, it will be a wonderful adventure.*

REFLECT AND LOOK AHEAD

Perhaps you will have opportunities to attend special events of your youth, especially ones that involve competition. Continue to let your youth know you want to be involved with them as they sort through how Jesus would have them handle competition. Be available for their questions.

DIGGING DEEPER

The wisdom of this world so often says that to succeed you need to look out for yourself, to view all others as competitors and challengers. The sad result is that loneliness has become a common experience in today's world. Often we bring it upon ourselves by our competitive attitudes towards much of life.

In many ways the book of Ecclesiastes is the story of a lonely man. Instead of finding joy in God and in godly relationships, the author looks for joy in the pursuit of knowledge, in entertainment, in hard work, in fame, and in wealth—all of which seem to leave him empty and alone. The tone of Ecclesiastes becomes increasingly more despairing, except for the abrupt and welcome section thrown into the middle of all this futility where the author deals with the need for friendship and cooperation (4:9-12).

The strength and power we need to succeed in both life and godliness are rarely found in individuals striving alone. The passage describes a few of the life activities where two people have an advantage over one who struggles alone. Throughout these four famous verses, the author is talking about two people, but it is the last phrase of this passage where the real gem surfaces: "A threefold strand is not quickly broken." When two people come together, they are not just two individuals. A third strand emerges as well. Neither individual would have discovered strength and power if each had continued in the competitive, me-first attitudes this world of ours is so famous for. In the wonderful fusion of cooperation, each can discover that it is their strength, together with the strength of another, that produces an even greater measure of strength.

The writer could have used any number of images to convey this same powerful truth (two oxen harnessed together, logs burning together in a fire, two and three engines on off-shore racing boats, four wheels on a car all being aligned to face the same direction, etc.). The point of these four verses seems to be this: If you want to make it through this hurly-burly life where everything changes faster and faster, true success will be found only in community where individuals bind themselves together for wisdom, strength, help, warmth, companionship, and comfort.

Following Jesus is a communal adventure. It is a journey that demands that we work together. It requires great personal sacrifice and patience, perseverance, and large doses of God's grace every day. It takes practice, commitment, and a genuine desire to grow in faith and service. Surprisingly, it is a process that we can be part of even as we participate in some of life's many competitions.

HANDOUTS
Adventure Together

ADVENTURE TOGETHER

Work together as a team to complete the following eight events.
You may do the events in any order you wish.

1. Find someone from another group who looks as though they need encouragement. Have your entire team give that person a shoulder rub at once. Have this encouraged person initial here:

_____

2. Link arms and attempt to hop on only one foot each, a distance of 7.3 feet. Have a non-biased witness initial here:

_____

3. Find somebody from another team who looks thirsty, and offer them a drink of water. If she or he accepts, the whole group must say in unison, "Sorry, I would if I could but I can't so I won't." Have the thirsty person initial here: _____

4. Have your entire team form two lines, face each other, and link arms. Have your lightest team member lie down on these linked arms. The entire team must walk like this a total of 16 feet without dropping the brave volunteer. Have a witness initial here:

_____

6. Find an adult and tell them that God loves her or him. Ask them to initial here:

_____

5. Find another team that looks as though they are struggling with a particular event. Cheer them on for five seconds. Have one of them initial here:

_____

7. Pick a Christmas carol and sing one verse of it together. Have someone who heard you initial here:

_____

8. Link arms and give yourselves a big group hug. Have your entire team initial here:

_____